Scotland
the
Grave

From ghoulies and ghosties
And long-leggedy beasties
And things that go bump in the night
Guid Lord, deliver us.

Old Scottish children's prayer

Murder murder, polis!
Three stairs up.
The wummin in the middle flair
Hit me wi' a cup.
The cup's a' broken,
Ma heid's a' cut
Murder murder, polis!
Three stairs up.

Traditional Glasgow skipping rhyme

Scotland the Grave

Jeff Fallow

WAVERLEY
BOOKS

This edition published 2010 by Waverley Books,
144 Port Dundas Road, Glasgow, G4 0HZ

Illustrations, text and layout design by and
© 2010 Jeff Fallow

A catalogue entry for this book is available
from the British Library.

ISBN 978-1-902407-47-0

Printed and bound in the EU

CONTENTS

8

DR JEKYLL AND MR HYDE

Scottish author Robert Louis Stevenson (1850-1894) published *Dr Jekyll and Mr Hyde* in 1886 — the story of a man who thinks that evil could be separated from good in human beings. He invents a chemical mixture to do so.

After drinking the potion he has invented, Doctor Jekyll, good by day, becomes the evil Mr Hyde by night. But the experiment goes wrong and Mr Hyde completely takes over Dr Jekyll's personality and the doctor loses control.

DEACON BRODIE

Ah well, that's another honest day's business over.

Stevenson is thought to have based his novel on the true story of Deacon Brodie, who was hanged in 1788.

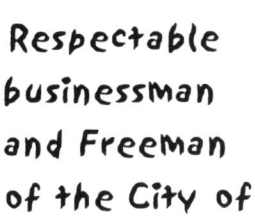

Respectable businessman and Freeman of the City of Edinburgh by day ...

It's getting dark outside.

William Brodie inexplicably became a desperate criminal and burglar by night.

Must...rob... must...steal.

His crimewave ended when he and his accomplices tried to rob the Excise Offices in Edinburgh's Canongate. One of the accomplices turned him and his fellow crooks in to the police. Brodie ran off to Europe but was arrested in Amsterdam, brought to Edinburgh for trial and was hanged near St Giles Cathedral, by, it is said, a device of his own invention.

DRACULA

Bram Stoker (1847–1912), Irish-born author of
Dracula, was supposedly inspired by a visit to a
Scottish Castle on a dark, stormy night. He visited
the ruined, tall-towered Slains Castle, overlooking
the jagged, rocky clifftops of Cruden Bay, near
Peterhead, in 1893.

The pounding waves, windswept cliffs, local tales
of ghosts and the vast, empty windows of the castle
created an atmosphere Stoker would bring to life
two years later in his classic vampire story.

FRANKENSTEIN'S MONSTER

Similarly, the bleak and atmospheric banks of the Firth of Tay near Dundee were to kindle the imagination of Mary Wollstonecraft Shelley (1797-1851), author of Frankenstein. Although English-born, Mary Shelley was brought up for many years in Scotland, and part of her novel is set there. Indeed, it is on the Orkney Islands that Dr Frankenstein creates his second monster, a female, a companion for his first creation.

Scotland, remember, is an ancient land, with tales and legends of spirits that go back to the Stone Age, when pagan stone circles and standing stones were established... OOPS!

PLOP

(Sorry about that). Anyway...

SHLUCK!

Let's not forget that the actual nation of Scotland was formed in the DARK AGES, a time of much bloodshed and superstition.

This provides a scenario for Shakespeare's MACBETH.

MACBETH

The real Macbeth wasn't really the bad guy that
Shakespeare's play suggests. In the play he tries
to use witchcraft and murder to stay in power.
The real Macbeth didn't actually murder anyone.
He killed King Duncan in battle; he didn't murder
him in cold blood.

Still, Shakespeare's Macbeth makes a good
story, a chilling tale of Scotland's serial killer
king and the three unforgettable witches. You've
probably heard the quote: "Double, double toil
and trouble, fire burn and cauldron bubble".

19

Over the centuries, the Scots fought the English, and the Scots fought each other.

Battles have stained the moors with blood, witch-burnings have blackened the air with smoke, and the dark Georgian streets of Edinburgh, and Victorian gaslit streets of Glasgow have hidden sinister secrets.

So welcome to "bony" Scotland. Pleasant dreams, everyone.

Chapter 1 : Ghosts

Haunted Places? Hundreds of 'em! Not surprising
really, that an ancient country like Scotland
abounds with ghosts. There's hardly a castle,
country hall or ruined abbey that doesn't have at
least one resident spirit and many - like Edinburgh
Castle, Glamis castle and Fife's Balgonie Castle -
have several.

   These days you are just as likely to see a ghost
in a modern suburb, a council flat, a supermarket, a

car park, a theatre or a hospital. Ghosts sightings are so numerous, in fact, that they can be divided into categories:

UNHAPPY SPIRITS

This group of restless dead would include the headless phantom of <u>Tynron Castle</u> in Dumfriesshire. He is said to be young MacMilligan of Balgarnock, who came to the castle to court the daughter of the great and powerful Lord McGachan. McGachan's sons thought poor MacMillagan no suitable partner for their sister and chased him on his horse right over the castle crag. As he fell down the cliff, his head was knocked off and his headless phantom still haunts the area.

Glamis Castle in Angus, ancestral home of the late Queen Mum's family, has supposedly more windows visible on the outside than there are on the inside, and more than its share of restless ghosts: Earl Beardie, though dead for over 500 years, still plays dice with the Devil. A grotesquely deformed illegitimate heir, with a huge, hairy, egg-shaped body, was supposed to have been kept in a secret room. A lunatic appears on the roof, a black page boy outside one of the bedrooms, and a woman with no tongue in the park. The Grey Lady of Glamis, Janet Douglas, burned as a witch in the 16th century, is seen amid the flames that devoured her either in the Chapel or in the clock tower. What a gang!

And these are just a few of the Ghosts of Glamis!

23

GREY, GREEN OR WHITE LADIES

Grey Ladies like Janet Douglas of Glamis, and indeed Green Ladies, are a common form of ghost in Scotland. The ruined MacDuff Castle at East Wemyss in Fife has a Grey Lady. She is the ghost of Mary Sibbald, who ran off with a Gypsy, was accused of theft, and flogged. She took ill and died, haunting the castle and the Wemyss Caves.

Fetteresso Castle near Stonehaven has a Green Lady, seen walking through the walls of the house and, on occasion, carrying a baby. Sometimes only her footsteps are heard. But, just to be different, some places have a White Lady, such as Edzell Castle in Angus. She is Catherine, second wife of Earl David of Crawford. She fell into a coma in 1578

GREEN WITH JEALOUSY

Grrr! I used to be a GREY lady before SHE stole all the attention!

and was buried alive, waking up in her exhumed coffin when someone tried to cut off her finger to steal her ring. Locked out of the castle, she died of exposure in the cold.

HARBINGERS OF DEATH

Spirits that appear when someone is about to die. <u>Wemyss Castle</u> at West Wemyss, Fife, has a resident ghost of this type. Lady Jean Wemyss, fondly known as Green Jean, walks the corridors of the great house whenever death is about to befall somebody.

During the First World War the house was used as a hospital for wounded soldiers, and Green Jean was seen a lot during this period.

Contachy Castle near Kirriemuir, Angus, is haunted by the sound of a phantom drummer whenever a person of the Clan Ogilvie is about to die. The drummer was a Cameron in Lord Ogilvie's service during the Covenanter Wars of the 17th century. He failed to beat the drum to warn of the enemy approaching, so was thrown into a fire.

HISTORICAL RE-ENACTMENTS

Some apparitions are not solitary figures, but ghostly groups acting out a scene that took place long ago, such as the marching armies that have sometimes been seen in foggy weather in Queen's Park in Glasgow. They are said to be the spectres of soldiers of the army of Mary, Queen of Scots on their way to fight those of the Earl of Moray at the Battle of Langside, 1568.

On the shores of Loch Ashie, near Inverness, a traveller on the moors during the First World War saw a battle without a sound. The soldiers, in Dark Ages costume, fought with sword, axe and spear, some on foot and some on horseback, all fighting fiercely in complete silence. Suddenly the whole scene vanished. The scene has been reported on several occasions, and local tradition has it that a

battle was fought in the area between Gaelic forces of Fionn MacCumhaill (pronounced Fin MacCool) and local Pictish tribes.

At <u>Brimmond Hill</u> near Aberdeen a phantom army, first recorded in 1643, has sometimes been seen passing through the mist and vanishing out of sight.

The northeast seems to be the 'in' place for phantom armies. In 1932, two boys, the Millar brothers, saw a ghostly army preparing for battle at Broad Hill on <u>Aberdeen Links</u> on a sunny summer's day. The huge army vanished without trace.

PHANTOM PIPERS

Inevitably, Scotland, land of the bagpipes, has many phantom pipers. For example, the Piper's Brae near <u>Culzean Castle</u> on the coast of Ayrshire is known to resound to the sound of phantom pipes whenever a head of the Kennedy family is about to be married, though the actual identity of the piper is a mystery.

At <u>West Wemyss</u> in Fife is a row of sea caves, home to cavemen, Picts and smugglers at different periods in history, called the Wemyss Caves. One of

the caves is called the Piper Cave because, legend has it, a drunken piper wandered into it after returning from a fair. He never came out again.

His pipes were heard, growing fainter as he wandered deeper in but, though a search was made for him, right to the end of the cave, he was never found.

A ghostly piper is said to Haunt Fort George, near Inverness. The fort was built in 1746 after the Battle of Culloden, when Bonny Prince Charlie's uprising against King George II failed. The Highlands remained under military occupation for nearly a century after Culloden, but the phantom piper to this day reminds everyone that the Highland spirit will never be broken.

STRANGE PHANTOMS AND ELEMENTAL SPIRITS

The most famous apparition in this category is the Big Grey Man of Ben MacDui. The mountain (4000 feet/1309 metres) is in the Cairngorms mountain range, 10 miles southeast of Aviemore in the remote Highlands, and the phantom has been recorded many times since the 19th century by reliable witnesses, both as unearthly footsteps and in visual form, said to be ten feet tall!

Meanwhile, the hills near <u>Bathgate</u> in West Lothian are said to be visited by a Silver Man. A family, describing what they saw as 'not silver, more like a negative image' of a person witnessed it on the road at Ravencraig Wood, its body glowing while it ran at the speed of a car!

ROAD PHANTOMS
There are ghosts that appear on the open road, usually seen at night on quiet country roads. Often they appear in front of cars, vanishing at what

should be the moment of impact. Fife seems to be a good area to spot them. On the <u>Kennoway</u> road from Leven, near Springfield cottages at the entrance to the Durie House driveway (a dark and lonely spot), a group of miners in old-fashioned working men's clothes have sometimes been sighted, and in 1997 a local man driving on that road saw what appeared to be a drunken figure in dark clothes walk in front of his car and suddenly vanish.

A similar thing happened in the 1960s on the <u>Cupar to St Andrews</u> road when a couple's car was followed by 'two moons'. Suddenly an old man walked in front of the car, collided without a sound, and vanished without trace.

GHOSTLY VEHICLES

Not all phantoms take human or animal shape. Machinery too, it seems, can take ghostly form. This raises the sometimes-asked question of whether spooks are necessarily spirits of the dead. They (or some of them anyway) could be a kind of visual 'echo' of light through time, just like the 'ghosting' effect you get on a faulty TV (which is a light-echo across space).

Ghostly aeroplanes (as well as ghostly pilots or

airmen) which appear then vanish into the air, have often been seen around the old abandoned aerodrome at <u>Montrose</u>, while a phantom lorry has been seen on several occasions – both by day and by night – on the Portree to Sconser road on the <u>Isle of Skye</u>.

The coach of the Wizard Laird, Alexander Skene (1680–1724) is said to haunt the area of <u>Loch Skene</u>, 10 miles west of Aberdeen. The Laird is said to have practised black magic and, according to legend, to have cast no shadow, which had been taken by the Devil. One night he is said to have crossed the frozen loch on his coach, followed by two black hounds. The ice broke and the hounds drowned, but the coach got across. The coach is still reportedly seen, drawn by four black horses.

OTHER SETTINGS

Castles, chapels, churchyards and Great Halls are
the traditional haunts of ghosts, but spooks can
turn up just about anywhere, it seems. An oil
worker on the <u>Ninian Southern oil platform</u> in the
North Sea in 1990 saw a spectral couple in 1920s
clothes, thought to be the victims of a yachting
disaster, while the former offices of the <u>Edinburgh
Evening News</u> in Edinburgh is the haunt of a
spectral printer in old-fashioned clothes.

A <u>supermarket</u> on <u>Elgin's High Street</u>, built on old
monastery grounds, is the haunt of mysterious tall
apparitions in black or white cloaks, disembodied
voices and poltergeist activity, witnessed during
closed hours by members of staff.

A <u>council flat</u> in the Sinclairtown area of
<u>Kirkcaldy</u>, Fife, was haunted for years in the late
1980s/early 1990s. A tenant of five years reported
ghostly disturbances and 'dancing lights', supported
by the complaints of the next tenant, a young
single man, who asked the local council to be
rehoused. There was nothing structurally wrong
with the flat, but there were mysterious sounds
and knockings (not from through the walls), there
were 'cold spots' and a faceless, amorphous, misty
apparition appearing in the bedroom. The council

seriously considered having an exorcism performed, though it never came about, but psychic investigators inspected the flat and the haunting received press and TV coverage in 1993.

Theatres are a popular haunt of spectres and spirits, and many theatres have their own resident ghost. Edinburgh's Festival Theatre, the Citizen's Theatre in Glasgow and the Byre Theatre in St Andrews are prime examples. Often, theatre ghosts are said to be the spirit of someone who threw himself or herself off the balcony.

Hospitals, too, are frequented by our ectoplasmic friends. Not surprising really, when you think about it. Gartloch hospital, just outside Glasgow, is a grim, fortresslike former mental hospital with twin Gothic towers. Home to a black-clad female figure, the building is now flats. Glasgow's Royal Infirmary, built next to the Necropolis (which we'll get to later) and the ancient medieval Glasgow Cathedral, is haunted by a Green Lady, a ghostly nurse, but she is a benevolent spirit, said to bring help. The Western Infirmary in Glasgow has many more modern additions than the Royal, but has old parts dating from 1871. It has a resident ghost, Sir William MacEwen (died 1924), who haunts one of the operating theatres.

So, when in Scotland, you're never far from a haunted place. Ghosts? The place is full o' them!

Chapter 2 : Witches

From the Middle Ages into the 18th century, witchcraft was a criminal offence in Scotland. Yet many communities had their own local white witch (called a goodwife in the Lowlands and a spey wife in the Highlands and Islands) who would mix herbal remedies, heal illnesses, ward off curses or evil spells, and tell fortunes. Their beliefs and practices were often a mixture of Christian ritual and ancient Celtic folklore.

But the most common idea of a witch that has passed into legend is the hag who put curses on

people, summoned power from the Devil, turned milk sour and mixed wicked potions containing toad's venom, animal body parts and other tasty goodies. Bad witches did exist, and did indeed meet in secret covens, but most people accused of witchcraft were completely innocent of causing harm.

TAM O'SHANTER

The poem Tam o'Shanter is Scotland's best-known witch tale, told by the national bard, Robert Burns (1759-1796), and based on an Ayrshire legend. Tam was a farmer from Alloway, Burns' home village, who was fond of a drink. One dark, stormy Saturday night as he was riding home drunk as usual, he was attracted by some kind of activity at Alloway's old haunted church. Looking through a window, he saw a macabre dance of witches and wizards while the Devil, in the form of a huge black dog, played on the bagpipes. Forgetting himself - and slightly tiddly - Tam shouts out:

> 'Weel done, cutty sark!'
> And in an instant, all was dark.

The ghostly crew notice him and give chase! They

intend to sacrifice him to the Devil! Tam flees on
his horse, Meg, to the Auld Brig o' Doon (which
witches would not cross). A witch grabbed Meg's
tail, which came off. Tam and his horse crossed the
bridge in time and escaped, but poor Meg was left
without a tail.

THE BLACKSMITHS AND THE WITCH
At <u>Yarrow</u>, near Selkirk, once lived two brothers,
both blacksmith's apprentices. Every night, a witch
would sneak up on the younger lad and put a magic
bridle over his head which turned him into a horse.
She would then ride him to the coven. When his big

brother found out about this, they switched places one night. The older brother was stronger, he swiped the bridle off the witch and put it on her, turning HER into a horse. After galloping around on her for miles, he took her to the smithy's workshop and shod her. Next morning, the witch had horseshoes attached to her feet and hands.

PROPHECIES

Some witches would tell the future, but sometimes the prophecy turned out in an unexpected way.

Just before the Battle of Banchory (1562), the witches of Strathbogie told the Earl of Huntly, Clan Chief of the Gordons, that after the battle he would lie in Aberdeen Tollbooth without a wound on his body. His clan were defeated in the battle by the troops of Mary, Queen of Scots, and Huntly was captured. But, although he wasn't wounded, he had a sudden attack of apoplexy (a funny turn) and fell off his horse. His (unwounded) dead body was laid in the Tollbooth, as prophesied.

CURSES

There are plenty of tales of witches putting curses on people, such as the three witches at Ardnamurchan who were found sticking pins into a curse doll of the Clan Chief of the MacLeans of Duart in the 17th century, causing pains throughout his body until a gentleman cattle-thief, MacIain Ghiass, chased off the witches and removed the pins.

Or the time when Sir Ewen Cameron of Lochiel was met by a local hag called Gormul as he was about to cross on the ferry at Ballachulish. 'Blessings on you, Ewen,' she cried out. 'Your blessings be on yonder grey stone,' Cameron replied, and the stone split in two. He knew what kind of blessings SHE meant!

(An interesting thing about Ballachulish, by the way: An ancient oak figure of a pagan Celtic goddess was found there. It is 5 feet tall, with quartz eyes, and surrounded by a wicker shrine. It can be seen in the National Museum of Antiquities in Edinburgh).

I CAN'T BELIEVE THEY WERE AFTER BUTTER

Witches were believed to be particularly fond of stealing milk or butter. They were blamed when cows failed to produce milk, and it was believed that a witch could steal milk by use of magic, such as turning herself (or himself) into a hare and suck milk from the cows. Every area had its own local method for fighting this kind of magic. In Fife, for example, you could reverse the spell and make your cows produce milk again if you made a rope out of cows' tail hair and skipped with it, saying 'Hare's milk and mare's milk, and all the beasts that bears milk, come to me!'

Hare's milk
And mare's milk
And all the beasts
that bears milk,
Come — to —
ME!!

SKIPPETY SKIP

On the Island of Tiree in the Inner Hebrides, the trick was to make a ball of hair called a 'ronag' every Lammas Eve (August 1) and put it on the milk pail. However, sometimes such charms didn't work unless the witch was bribed. At Crawick, Dumfriesshire, the maid at the manse noticed that the churned cream wouldn't turn to butter, and

told the minister. They tried the usual tricks –
carrying the churn over a stream, tying sprigs of
rowan to it, hanging horseshoes on the door of the
cowshed, but only when the minister's wife gave
the local witch a present of a piece of butter did
the trouble stop.

WHITE WITCHES AND WISE WOMEN
But of course, not all witches used magic for
harmful purposes. As said earlier, many communities
had their own local white witch, goodwife, spey
wife or Wise Woman. In Torridon in the far north, a
visitor at the end of the 19th century reported a
miraculous cure when a man repairing a horse's
harness stuck a needle in his hand. The spey wife,
who was sitting watching, pulled out the needle
and uttered a charm:

> Be your poison within the ground
> May your pain be within the hill
> Wholeness be to the wound
> Rest be to the hurt.

Not only did the bleeding stop immediately, but
the wound healed instantly without trace.

Not all witches were women either. Grigor Willox was a well known healer in the area of Tomintoul (the highest village in Britain), in the northeast, in the 18th century.

People travelled for long distances to see him and he practised all over the north of Scotland, curing the sick, breaking evil spells or curses and tracing thieves by magical means. He was thought to possess part of a kelpie's bridle (a kelpie is a water spirit – we'll come to that later) as a magical tool.

WITCH HUNTS

Stories, folk tales and legends aside, there was a grim side to witchcraft, and that was punishment and persecution. For centuries, witchcraft was an offence carrying the death penalty. Why?

1) A way of keeping women 'in their place'

Women who weren't afraid to fly.

If a man had a score to settle, he could turn to the law. For centuries, women couldn't, so they might try putting a curse on someone who had offended them.

2) A way of keeping the lower classes in their place

Treason and rebellion against the rulers of the country, people were told, was the work of the Devil. People were told to look out for the Devil and his followers everywhere. Turn people against witches, the ruling classes thought, and they won't turn against their masters.

3) Fear

It was believed that people really could use magic to control nature or interfere with people's lives, and that this power came from the Devil.

Some periods were worse than others. In Scotland, the reign of King James VI was the worst period of witch-hunting, followed in the 17th century by the time of the Covenanters.

Where's that Devil?

Town halls and towers like the Tollbooth at Glasgow Cross became jails for accused witches. Nearly half of all those accused were executed.

CONFESS!

Around 1,350 witches were killed in Scotland – three times as many as in England. At Gallow Hill, two miles north of the village of Skalloway in Shetland, black ash from numerous witch-burnings can still be found in the soil, while at Forfar Museum you can see a 17th century 'witches' bridle' – an iron gag put on the witch on her way to execution to stifle her screams.

Helen Guthrie met her end in this way after confessing to eating babies (she thought that by confessing things she might escape torture).

48

One of the last Scottish witches burned at the stake was Janet Horne, executed at Dornoch in 1722. She was charged with turning her daughter into a pony.

But the uncrowned queen of all the Scottish witches was Isobel Gowdie (d. 1760) from Auldearn on the Moray Firth. Her coven of 13 met in the hills and cursed the Laird of Park's children by throwing dolls made to look like them into a fire.

They tried to do the same with the Laird of Lochloy's family, spreading stewed dog flesh (said to have been stirred by the devil himself) along their paths. But the family must have taken a detour, because the spell failed.

Isobel Gowdie cheerfully admitted all this and more, claiming to have visited the land of Sibh (the Celtic magic 'Otherworld', pronounced 'Shee'), and to have been shown how to make poison elf-arrows by the fairy Queen of Sibh. She also claimed that she and her coven could transform themselves into hares, cats or jackdaws.

The spell for changing into a cat involved saying three times over:

> I shall go into ane cat
> With sorrow and such and a black shot
> And I shall go in the Devil's name
> And will I come home again.

Changing back to human form also required repeating a charm. Here's one Isobel Gowdie used to change from hare back to human:

> Hare, hare, God send thee care!
> I am in a hare's likeness now
> But I shall be woman even now
>   Hare, hare, God send thee care!

WICCANS
Modern witches call themselves Wiccans. Wicca is a nature-worshipping religion and many of its followers – such as Hedge Witches or Kitchen Witches – use saucepans rather than cauldrons, in

Where's the fun in that?

which they stew herbs, make natural remedies and cook vegetarian recipes instead of tongue of toad and eye of newt. Have you ever tried to buy toad tongues? You won't find them in your local supermarket. Not even in the freezer section.

Chapter 3 : The North Berwick Witches

King James VI (who would become James I of England) ruled Scotland as a tyrant. He had political and religious enemies all around him and he felt insecure, becoming more and more strict and intolerant of those who disagreed with him. Assassination attempts were made on him, such as Guy Fawkes' failed Gunpowder Plot of 1605, celebrated today on Bonfire Night every 5th of November.

A TORTUOUS TALE OF TREASON

But the strangest attempt on James' life was in 1590, allegedly using sorcery and witchcraft.

The source of this threat to the king was the king's cousin Francis Hepburn, Earl of Bothwell. How did they find this out? They tortured some 'witnesses'. Do you think you can count on statements made under torture?

Bothwell was next in line to the Scottish throne and, should James die without a child, he would be king. It was said that Francis led a coven of witches by dressing up as the Devil and allowing his own body to become possessed.

Suits me, don't you think?

The first torture victim in the case was Gilly Duncan, maidservant to David Seaton, the Deputy Baillif of the East Lothian village of Tranent.

Baillif Seaton noticed Gilly sneaking out every night without permission and became suspicious. Gilly was becoming well known locally as a wise-woman and a healer (the authorities viewed

54

these women as witches). Seaton had her tortured
with thumbscrews (charmingly called 'pilnie-winks'
in Scotland at that time. Sounds like a children's
game, doesn't it?), but she confessed nothing. So
the authorities brought her in for further
questioning and, when they found a mole growing
on her throat, that was all the proof they needed.
The Devil's Mark, they called it.

In their view she was clearly a witch, and
tortured her some more. This time she talked. She
said Bothwell had a plot to use witches to sink the
king's ship ...

THE CURSE ON THE KING ... AND THE CAT

On the pier at Leith (Edinburgh's port), a coven of witches from North Berwick cast a spell out to sea to raise a storm and sink the king's ship. They saw the royal ship, carrying James and his bride Anne of Denmark, returning home from their wedding in Norway. One of the witches held a cat with blobs of human flesh, cut from a hanged man's body, tied to

(DISCLAIMER: This spell is not guaranteed fail-proof!) (Aw, frigate!)

its paws. As the hags cried out their spell, the poor wailing moggie was hurled into the Firth of Forth.

A storm brewed up immediately. The sky darkened with clouds, howling winds swept and huge waves battered. A boat crossing from Fife was sunk with all its crew ... but the royal ship reached harbour safely after a rough voyage up the Firth.

AGNES SAMPSON
Agnes Sampson, a midwife and well known magical and herbal healer, was one of those who confessed under torture. After the failed attempt to sink the king's ship, she asked one of his servants for a

piece of cloth which had been worn by him. She planned to wipe toad's venom all over it and put a curse on King James so that he'd die in agony. The servant refused to give her the linen. So the witches met up one night at Prestonpans and passed a wax effigy of the king from hand to hand, chanting their curse ...

... but that didn't work either.

THE DEVIL GOES TO NORTH BERWICK
On Hallowe'en, 1590, Agnes confessed that up to 200 drunken witches met the Devil at North Berwick Kirk. She said a young schoolmaster, Dr John Fian from Saltpans, was Satan's secretary, taking notes as the Devil preached from the pulpit, surrounded by black candles. Arriving at the church on a black horse with flaming torches attached to its head, Fian kept a list of all who attended the Great Coven, and made them each take an oath of loyalty to his master. Gilly Duncan played a jews harp as the coven danced and swirled around, singing their chant:

> Cummer*, go ye before,
> Cummer go ye.
> If ye will not go before,
> Cummer, let me.

(*cummer = sister)

The Devil, with black gown, great glowing eyes, hairy clawed feet and hands and a huge beaked nose, preached about obedience to himself to bring down King James.

THE TRIAL

Four people were brought to trial: Dr Fian, Agnes Sampson, Barbara Napier and the daughter of Lord Cliftonhall, Euphemia MacLean.

Dr Fian was tortured with an apparatus called 'the boot', a boot-shaped metal vice that fitted over the foot, crushing it slowly as a tightening screw was turned. He told his captors all about the coven but that night, alone in his cell, the Devil appeared to him with a white wand (or so he told his jailers the next morning). Satan snapped the wand and said: 'When you die, you are mine'.

But, even with the boot again, the tortured teacher kept quiet and said no more.

The three others were tortured too, but King James got bored with them, calling them liars and ordering their execution for wasting his time.

Agnes had a plan – she hoped to prove that they weren't lying, hoping for a respite. She told King James what his wife said to him when they were alone on the ship, something only James could have

61

known. Satisfied that they weren't liars, he ordered them executed as witches.

Agnes and Euphemia were executed on Castle Hill. Barbara Napier was also condemned, but was freed later. Dr Fian was put to death on Castle Hill in January 1591, first by being strangled and then finished off by being burned at the stake.

Francis, Earl Bothwell, ran off to Italy. All his money was gone. He spent the rest of his life in Naples practising the Black Arts, they say, until he died in 1624.

Chapter 4 : Michael Scott

Great writers and poets of history, such as Boccaccio and Sir Walter Scott, have written poems and stories about Michael Scott, Scotland's greatest wizard. But who was Michael Scott in real life? He was an astrologer (and doctor, and personal advisor) to Frederick II, Emperor of the Holy Roman Empire.

LIFE STORY

Michael Scott was born around 1175 in Oakwood Tower near Melrose in the Scottish Borders. He attended Roxburgh Grammar School and then studied at Oxford and Paris.

The Pope offered him the job of Bishop of Cashel in Ireland, but he turned it down because he couldn't speak Irish Gaelic!

He taught and further studied at Padua and other Italian cities until he was offered the job of private tutor to Prince Frederick, who was then just a young boy. Scott was a father-figure to the lad, whose own father, 'Barbarossa', had died in battle.

When the prince grew up, Scott went to Toledo to study zoology, natural history and the works of the great Arab scholars of the day. He translated certain works of the Greek philosopher Aristotle, which might have been lost forever if it weren't for Michael Scott.

MAGIC!

But also at Toledo he studied astrology, alchemy and, it was thought, occult magic. Frederick, an open believer in such things, had now become Emperor of the Holy Roman Empire, and offered his old master and mentor the position as his personal astrologer. So Scott remained astrologer and doctor to his former pupil until he retired.

On his retirement, Scott returned to Scotland, spending his time hunting or riding on his lands in the Borders or at Balwearie Castle, Fife, which he inherited from his mother's side of the family. Even in retirement, his services were called upon by the

65

King, Alexander III, who asked him to act as ambassador to France, granting him a knighthood.

Scott died around 1250. His place of burial is unknown, but somewhere in the grounds of Melrose Abbey seems most likely. His life story is interesting enough, but the legends and stories that grew up around him are fascinating...

THE CAT GIRL

In Italy, a young aristocratic woman came to visit the wiz, wanting to know how to turn herself into a cat. Scott explained what to do. She should burn a certain herb with magical properties, utter a spell and concentrate on leaving her own body and entering the prepared skin of a cat.

So off she went with cat skin, herb burner and spell parchment. But she used the magic for wrongful purposes, killing her ex-boyfriend (who had left her to marry another woman), together with his wife and young son by sinking her cat fangs into their throats while they slept.

Meanwhile, the cat-girl's little brother had seen a cat with no eyes leave his sister's room and had told their parents. They found her lying in her room in a deathlike trance. They chased the cat around the house until it ran into the young woman's room, where they found her lying panting for breath beside the empty cat skin.

Realising what her daughter had done, the girl's mum threw the skin, the cooking pot and, finally, the young lady herself into the River Arno!

TIME TRAVEL

Another story tells of how Scott, at the coronation feast of Frederick, magically transported a German baron to a mysterious western land (undiscovered America). After 20 years there, the baron is magically returned by Scott to the dinner table, back to the moment he left.

Most stories about Michael Scott take place after his return to Scotland...

REVENGE OF THE WHELK!

Scott and his assistant were riding through the Fife countryside. They felt hungry, but were miles from Balwearie Castle, so Scott sent his assistant to a nearby farmhouse to ask the farmer's wife if she could spare a piece of bread. She lied, saying she had none, even though she was cooking bread and had plenty. So Scott placed a charmed whelk or 'buckie' over the front door. When the wife came outside, she started babbling:

'Sir Michael Scott's man
Sought bread and got nane'

over and over again, dancing wildly. The farmer and a farm girl joined her, caught up in the spell. They danced faster and faster until they all fell down exhausted and Scott removed the charm.

THE HARE AND THE HOUND

Also in Fife, Sir Michael had an arrangement with an old woman tenant that she could live rent-free as long as she would sometimes let him turn her into a hare for hunting purposes (he would never actually harm her, of course, only

70

chase her). But one day the dog handlers introduced a new hound without telling Scott. The dog almost caught the hare and would have killed her, but the wizard returned her to her human state just in time. After that, the old woman walked with a limp.

Later, at Oakwood in the Borders, Scott got a taste of what it was like to be turned into a hare himself when the local Witch of Fauldshope put a spell on him. His own dogs chased him but he was able to hide long enough to change himself back into a human.

(Hares were believed to be bringers of bad luck in those days, though hare's milk was believed by witches to have very powerful magical properties).

A MAGIC HOST

Michael Scott's wizard powers were known throughout Europe. When entertaining guests, he once provided a feast for them by conjuring up great dishes of food – out of the air! – from the kitchens of European kings.

THE BOOK OF MIGHT

Michael Scott kept his greatest magic secrets, it is said, in a great black leather-bound book called <u>De Tribus Impostoribus</u>, but which was more commonly called <u>The Book of Might</u>.

One day his assistant was asked to fetch the book from another wizard who had borrowed it, and to bring it back to Balwearie Castle. The assistant was forbidden to look at the book as it was dangerous for those who lacked training in or understanding of such things, but he couldn't resist a peek.

Walking along the Kennoway Road, the assistant opened the book and was immediately driven to madness, his body and arms flailing about as invisible demons, fiends and magic powers overwhelmed him. His master was sent for and Scott controlled the powers, freeing the assistant. (A bit like the Sorceror's Apprentice, really.)

SCOTT STOPS PIRATES

King Alexander of Scotland, as already mentioned, called on the Master Wizard to act as ambassador to France, the reason being that French pirates were attacking and robbing Scottish ships in the Firth of Forth. Legend has it that Michael Scott not only rode but FLEW over to France on his great black demonic horse to meet the French king.

When the King of France refused to do anything about it, Scott ordered his steed to stamp on the floor.

CRASH ... DING DONG ... DING DONG!!

One stamp of its mighty hoof rang every bell in Paris, but still the king would not agree

73

74

to take action against the pirates. The wizard then ordered the amazing horse to stamp its hoof a second time.

CRRRRACK!!!

The second stamp sent cracks along every wall, floor and roof throughout the city.

Earth-shattering stuff!

As the fearsome steed raised its hoof for a third stamp the French king, fearing destruction of the city, backed down and promised to stop the piracy. Scott then flew back to Edinburgh and was knighted by King Alexander.

THE EILDON HILLS

An exciting story from the Borders tells how the three Eildon Hills came into being by way of Michael Scott's magic.

Using his Book of Might, Michael Scott decided he wanted to conjure up a powerful demon. He was hoping he could make it carry out useful tasks for himself.

First he had to test its power. He thought a worthy task woud be to break the Eildon Hill (which up until then had been a single cone) into the three hills we see today.

With an incantation he told the demon to do

his bidding. With a rupturous earthquake, the demon cracked the mountain into three.

The three parts drew away from each other, leaving a gap in the middle.

But the powerful demon remained restless.

ROPES FROM SAND

The demon demanded greater tasks, driving the magician mad with feelings of mental anguish, pain and torment.

The wise wizard, however, outsmarted the fiend by giving it an impossible task that would never be completed.

At Ringdoo Point on the Solway Firth, he ordered it to make ropes out of sand. The devil tried every day to do this, but at high tide its work would be washed away, so that it would have to start again the next day.

Scott was mercifully rid of the demon but, according to legend, it still tries vainly to carry out its task to this day, and at Ringdoo Point you can see the twisted, rope-like shapes in the sand.

78

PREDICTIONS

Michael Scott, it is said, could even predict when people would die.

He predicted the death of Emperor Frederick at the gates of a town called 'Flora'. Frederick, thinking it must be Florence, avoided that city, but died at a town called Fiorentino, in a bed in a building by the old town gates.

Scott also predicted the death of King Alexander by being thrown from his horse.

To avoid this, the king had his horse put to

death and got another one. But the next year the new horse, catching sight of the bones of the old one, reared up in alarm, throwing the king off and causing him to break his neck.

Finally, Sir Michael even forecast his own death by a falling rock. To prevent this, he devised an iron helmet but, taking it off to pray at Melrose Abbey, a loose block fell on him.

No one knows where the body of Michael Scott lies, but it is said that his Book of Might is buried with him.

The site of Oakwood Tower is now home to Sir David Steel, and very little remains of Balwearie Castle. But if you visit Melrose Abbey, you can see an old stone carving of Scott, the great wizard, created as a memorial to him.

Chapter 5 : Creatures of the Darkness

Do you like cats? Some people find them scary, with their big, staring eyes and their claws.

I must admit I'm quite fond of them, even though they won't do as they're told and can be a pain in the neck at times. Cats were worshipped in ancient Egypt and, as every cat owner knows, the cheeky moggies have never quite forgotten this. The pet cat is descended from the African wild cat (felis lybicus), which could at least be tamed. The Scottish wild cat or wildcat (felis sylvestris grampius), however, can't be tamed. If faced, it can be very fierce.

THE CATSHEE

But no flesh-and-blood wildcat is as fierce as the terrible supernatural CATSHEE.

No, not the she-cat. The Catshee.

'Catshee' comes from the Gaelic 'Cat Sibh', which means 'fairy cat'. But 'fairy' here does not describe cute little people with lacy wings. The Sibh was the Otherworld of ancient pagan belief, the realm of supernatural beings and spirits. So Catshee might be better translated as 'ghost cat' or even 'demon cat'. But we'll come back to the Catshee soon.

THE BANSHEE

Perhaps you have heard of the BANSHEE? ('Fairy Woman' or 'Otherworld Woman' in Gaelic), usually in tales from Ireland, right in there with leprechauns and green Irish fairies.

Well, Highland Scotland has the Banshee too. She's a fearsome, vampire-type hag, a stealer of souls who appears when someone is about to die, screeching out her terrifying death-scream in the night, her wild hair and long trailing robes floating out behind her as she sails through the air.

THE COOSHEE

There is also the Cooshee (Cu Sibh), the monstrous, green-glowing phantom dog of the Highlands.

A real hound from Hell, this is not the sort of mutt you want want to get to fetch a stick. The size of a pony, this devil dog stalks its victims silently, then bares its fangs in a low growl, with pools of saliva forming at its feet. Wherever the

terrified victim tries to run, the mad mutt chases
them into a bog, swamp or pool to drown.

THE BOOBRIE BIRD

There is the enormous Boobrie Bird, which lives in
the West Highland Lochs and carries off cows to
eat them.

THE NUCKLE-A-VEE
Some are even more grotesque. The Nuckle-a-vee is
half human, half horse. Unlike a Greek centaur

84

(which has the head and shoulders of a human on a horse's body), this thing walks upright on human legs and has long arms and a horse's head. It has no skin and appears in hideous form with with all its muscles, veins, sinews and arteries showing. Luckily, it hates fresh water, so you can escape from it by crossing a stream or loch.

THE HEADLESS TRUNK

Or there's the Headless Trunk (Coliunn Gun Cheann), a monstrous form without a head that used to haunt the grounds of Morar House, near Loch Morar, tearing passers-by from limb to limb. That was until a member of the MacDonald Clan beat the monster in battle and sent it packing.

OTHER SPIRITS

Some evil spirits are widespread, such as the Ciuthach, which haunts caves throughout the Highlands.

Others are local to a specific place, such as the
<u>Cuachag</u>, a water demon that lurks in Loch Cuaich,
Inverness-shire, or the <u>Baist Bheulach</u> that haunts
Odail Pass in Skye. This night-wailing demon is a
shape-shifter, able to change form at will to bring
down disaster to all who meet it.

Old Border castles are said to be the haunt of
local evil spirits called '<u>the Dunters</u>' ('hitters'),
whose legend is said to go back to ancient pagan
times of human sacrifice. The Dunters are supposed
to be the spirits of sacrificial victims.

Even worse are their evil elvish cousins, '<u>the
Red Cap</u>', who also haunt old Border castles and,
after killing their victims, dip their caps in the
blood to make them red.

SEA PEOPLE

Meanwhile, out in the Western Isles, <u>the Blue Men</u> of the Minch come up from their undersea caves, where they live in clans, to cause shipwrecks. And speaking of sea people ...

Around the islands of the far North, Orkney and Shetland, <u>selkies</u> take the form of seals while they live in the sea, but transform into human shape when they come up on land.

Selkies, however, are not evil or malicious, and even intermarry with humans or mortals.

HARMLESS SPIRITS

Similarly, <u>the Brown Man</u> of the Moors, a guardian nature spirit, is not evil, though he may use violence to protect wildlife. A kind of supernatural animal rights activist, he guards the wild animals of the Scottish Borders. He is usually seen dressed in brown, with a great bush of red hair and mad, staring eyes.

The Tarrans of Aberdeenshire and the northeast are not actually evil either, but they are disturbed and unhappy and therefore bring unhappiness. They appear as mysterious lights and are supposed to be the spirits of babies who died before being baptised.

BRINGERS OR FORETELLERS OF DEATH

On the other hand, the Slaugh in the Highlands are spirits of evil people – the 'unforgiven dead'. Restless and unhappy, the Slaugh are very dangerous, seeking to harm and cause death.

Some spirits do not set out to bring about death, but to foretell death, letting people know when someone is about to die. The Banshee does this, for example, but there are others besides.

There is the Bodach, for example, a vague, grey manlike form who often appeared to clan members in times past whenever someone in the clan was about to die.

Or his female equivalent Caoineag (The Weeper), who would appear at the bottom of a waterfall, wailing into the night with her awful howl whenever death or disaster was about to befall the clan.

THE CATSHEE AGAIN

So, if traditional legend is anything to go by, Scotland's countryside is rich in terrifying horrors, not least the Catshee.

The Catshee itself is as big as a deerhound and is black all over except for a white spot on its breast. It hunts silently, then appears out of

nowhere to stand on a rock, hillside or tree stump, its lips drawn back in a snarl of terror, flaunting its fangs in a macabre grin of death. The hackles on its back bristle as if with electricity, its claws are ready to tear its prey apart, its eyes glow like burning coals and its ears are pulled back in menace.

Scotland, like other parts of Britain, from time to time has rumoured sightings of big cats described as resembling pumas, panthers or lynxes prowling the countryside. The Beast of Bodmin Moor in England is an example, where people reported seeing a panther-like animal, and Scotland has reports of similar sightings. Fife, in particular, has many reports of big cats being seen in the fields and hills. But these cats are believed to be flesh-and-blood, mortal creatures, exotic pets accidentally released into the wild.

The Catshee, however, is not mortal but supernatural. While big cat rumours are a modern legend of the last few decades, belief in the Catshee goes back many centuries.

If you DO meet the Catshee, the best thing to do is to keep still until it gives up on you and slinks off.

You see, it can't actually touch you, but for you to run away is exactly what it wants, as it will chase you to your doom in a swamp or loch.

Chapter 6 :
Major Thomas Weir

In the 1600s there was civil war in Scotland and England between the armies of the King (who wanted to be head of the Church) and the Puritans (who wanted the Church to be run by ordinary members). In England, the Puritan armies were led by Oliver Cromwell. In Scotland, Oliver Cromwell had followers too, and they were called Covenanters.

Thomas Weir (1600–1670) was an officer in the Covenanter army, fighting against the army of King Charles I from 1641.

Weir came from a good Lanarkshire family and in 1649 became Commander of Edinburgh Town Guard. He was in charge of the execution of the Marquis of Montrose, an important supporter of the King.

Perhaps the memory of this later haunted him.

Did he feel guilty about this? Did it make him feel bad? Perhaps we'll never know.

ODD BEHAVIOUR

Weir never married, but shared his house at the top of West Bow, Edinburgh, with his sister Jane (born 1610), who was sometimes known as 'Grizel' (some sources refer to her as Jean or Janet).

Over the years, his behaviour became odd. Whenever he met anyone, he waved his strangely-shaped black stick around and uttered exorcisms, charms and incantations.

Yet when he didn't have his stick, neighbours reported, his powers of fancy speech left him.

He told leading citizens and his friends in the Church that he was a wizard and belonged to a witchcraft sect. They refused to believe him.

The Provost of the city sent doctors to check him out, but it seemed clear from their investigations that the major was not mad.

Thomas, it seemed, was of sound mind.

MAJOR WEIR CONFESSES

Nevertheless, he confessed to being a servant of the Devil. His whole life, he claimed, had been full of disgusting acts of crime, and that his sister had helped him all along.

Grizel was not married. A schoolteacher from Dalkeith, it was said by locals that she practised witchcraft in the house with her brother.

One neighbour said they saw, in Stinking Close (a lane near Weir's house), a ten-foot tall woman laughing, surrounded by various phantoms, all laughing along with the giant spectre.

96

ARRESTED

Eventually, Thomas and Grizel were arrested by the Lord Provost of Edinburgh, and Weir himself was quite willing and cooperative. He made a full confession of terrible practises and witchcraft.

He was not at all ashamed, telling the court that what he had already told them was not even a hundredth part of all the crimes and witchcraft practices he'd committed.

Raising the dead, using demons to serve his will, making spells granting eternal life on Earth, even Grizel's ability to spin incredible amounts of yarn on her spinning wheel, were just a tiny fraction of what he managed to do using magic and witchcraft.

THE STICK

At their arrest, Grizel told the guards to make sure they took Thomas's stick. It was a gift from the Devil, she said, and was the source of all his magical power. It would answer the door, go shopping for him and clear the streets when he was out walking, running in front of the Major and whacking anyone who was in the way. Grizel confessed to being in league with the Queen of the Fairies and that both she and her brother could fly through the air.

99

EXECUTION

The poor old Major was strangled until almost dead, then burned just outside the city walls. His stick was burned with him, and a witness said that it twisted and turned strangely and took a long time to burn, just like its master.

Poor Grizel was hung on the Grassmarket. She tried to strip her clothes off, so the executioner kicked the hanging-ladder away quickly.

And yet the strange thing is, Thomas Weir was never actually formally charged with witchcraft!

GHOSTS

For a century after the deaths of Thomas and Jane Weir, no-one would dare enter their house, which was said to be haunted. The Major's cloaked ghost, complete with his magic stick, was seen in the midnight streets. The house itself glowed with eerie lights, and sounds of laughter were heard inside.

And even to this day, the tapping of the Major's stick and the blackened face of his sister have been reported around the area of Edinburgh's Grassmarket.

Chapter 7 :
Burke and Hare

In early 19th-century Edinburgh, there were plenty of people who wanted to make a career for themselves - one way or another. In the New Town, north of Princes Street, lived the wealthy people: merchants and professionals, businessmen, lawyers, doctors ... doctors who needed fresh corpses to study or to use for teaching their students.

In the Old Town, south of Princes Street, the city's poor crowded into the tall slum tenements.

BODY SNATCHERS!

In the dark, narrow lanes and closes prowled grave robbers and body snatchers, ready to dig up the newly-buried dead to sell them to certain doctors. Doctors who wanted to make their career in a competitive profession. Doctors who didn't ask questions about where the corpses came from. Doctors like Robert Knox, 'the boy who bought the beef' (see page 114).

Dr Knox was Edinburgh University's most prominent lecturer in anatomy, but he needed freshly dead human bodies to carry out his research.

104

The law had already limited the supply of dead bodies for medical research (cadavers), and iron railings were placed over graves in Greyfriars Churchyard, Edinburgh's most prominent cemetery.

Night watchmen were also hired to guard the graveyard by night.

A NEW SOURCE ...

So Messrs. Burke and Hare found a new way to get bodies to sell: MURDER! And they had a regular client ready to buy the bodies without asking where they came from – Dr Knox.

William Hare (born 1792) came over to Scotland from County Tyrone in Ireland. After working on the Union Canal, street peddling and taking a series of labouring jobs, he met his partner-in-crime, William Burke, who kept a seedy lodging-house in Edinburgh. When they heard that Dr Knox paid handsomely for each corpse, they turned to grave-robbing. But, of course, the newly-buried dead were becoming better guarded and protected.

Then, in December 1827, a man who lived in Burke's lodging took ill and died. Burke and Hare swapped his body in the coffin for a weighted sack. The coffin was buried – nobody but Burke and Hare knew where the real body was – and the corpse was sold to Dr Knox for Seven Pounds Ten Shillings (£7.50) – quite a lot in those days. From then on, they took to actually murdering people.

All the victims were poor, homeless, destitute or unemployed – people who Burke and Hare thought wouldn't be missed anyway.

They thought up a way to kill their victims without a mark, making the death look natural. They would offer the victim drink, get them drunk till he or she fell unconscious, then smother them.

107

Dr Knox may have had his suspicions, but if he did he said nothing, and Burke and Hare made a deal with him: £8 per body in the summer season, £10 in winter.

Over the next year, they murdered 16 people:

1   An old drunk woman from Gilmerton whom Hare found walking the streets.

2   An English street peddlar.

3   Joe, an old miller.

4 & 5 Mary Haldane and daughter.

6 & 7 An old Irish woman and her grandson.

8 A dustbinman (called a cinder-gatherer in those days).

9 An old woman being held by the police (Burke and Hare pretended they knew her and would take her home).

10 Mary Patterson.

11 A wandering woman from the countryside.

12 A girl named Ann McDougal (a relative of Burke's partner).

13 Mrs Ostler, a washerwoman.

14 James Wilson ('Daft Jamie'), a simple-minded fellow.

15 A girl Hare murdered by himself.

16 A woman named Campbell or Docherty (she used both names).

But things went wrong for the terrible two.

THEIR PLAN UNRAVELS

Students attending Dr Knox's anatomy class began to recognise the bodies. Some were those of people they'd seen walking the streets, alive and well, only hours before. After the 16th victim, the law were called in to do a search of Knox's labs, where they found the latest freshly-murdered body.

Burke and Hare were arrested, along with Hare's wife Margaret and Burke's partner Helen McDougal. So the Lord Advocate, Sir William Rae, offered Hare a deal: he would let Hare go if he gave evidence against Burke.

Helen McDougal and Margaret Hare also escaped

conviction as the charges against them were not proven.

EXECUTION

On Wednesday 28th January 1829, Burke was hanged at the top of Liberton's Wynd, not far from where he and Hare carried out their crimes. A huge mob of between 32,000 and 40,000 angry people came to see. As Burke was being hung, they shouted "He'll see Daft Jamie soon!"

As he dropped, the crowd cheered. The atmosphere was like that of a carnival, some ladies even turning out in summer dresses in bright colours.

After the hanging, Burke's body was given to the College of Surgeons for dissection. But riots broke out by students and people demanding to see the corpse, so it was put on public display for a day before being used for medical study.

Daft Jamie's mum tried to get Hare convicted as well, but the law insisted that he was free, so he ran off to London, where he is said to have died penniless in 1859.

Dr Knox was never prosecuted, but the Edinburgh mob stoned his house and burned a dummy of him. He moved to Glasgow, then to London, where he died in 1862.

According to some sources, students stole bits of Burke's skin and had them tanned and preserved. A pocket book, allegedly bound in Burke's skin, was sold to a professor who presented it to the Anatomical Museum of the New University. It still exists, and the cover looks like dark leather, stamped in gold letters: BURKE'S SKIN, 1829.

Can you judge THIS book by its cover?

A children's rhyme appeared at the time, and for many years afterwards children would chant in the streets:

Down the close and up the stair,
But and ben with Burke and Hare,
Burke's the butcher, Hare's the thief,
Knox the boy that buys the beef.

Chapter 8 :
It's a Knockout!

Edinburgh, city of Burke and Hare, was not the only place to witness body-snatchers (or 'resurrectionists', as they were often called). It happened in other places too. In Aberdeen they were known as 'Burkers'. In early 19th-century Glasgow the city's most exclusive graveyard, the Necropolis (it means 'City of the Dead') had iron railings put over the graves and had to be guarded. But poorer cemeteries were less well protected.

Some resurrectionists were especially daring and cheeky.

TAXI!

The Glasgow Herald (September 11, 1829) reports that two men hired a cab (or a 'noddy' as it was known) at Glasgow Cross and ordered the coachman to take them to Little Govan, but to stop at Gorbals Churchyard on the way. The passengers nipped into the graveyard with two shovels and a big sack, got back in the cab with the sack well-filled and asked the driver to drive on. The coachman

116

guessed what they'd been up to and drove them straight to the police station.

The police looked in the bag and found two bodies – a man and a woman.

A PROFITABLE TRADE

Body-snatching was quite a profitable trade. Doctors, desperate for bodies for the dissecting table, would pay anything from £5 to £30 for them, depending on requirements.

At a time when many honest, law-abiding working folk earned threepence (2p) a day, this was quite a lot of money!

STUDENTS!

Not all resurrectionists were vagabonds and street-criminals. Some were medical students!

Ramshorn Churchyard was close to the students' quarters of Glasgow University, and

This'll help pay my college fees!

£20

students would draw lots to decide who would dig up a corpse or two.

The last straw came when students desecrated the grave of a well-known beautiful woman, a Mrs McAlister, wife of a famed Glasgow haberdasher (her brother discovered that her grave had been disturbed). An angry mob attacked University buildings, smashing windows and demanding justice.

An official search was made, and parts of human bodies – including bits of Mrs McAlister – were found. The students responsible were sent to Edinburgh to stand trial, but were acquitted.

However, the ringleader, Granville Sharp Pattison, was so hated in Glasgow that he fled to America – where he became an eminent surgeon!

118

CHLOROFORM

Scotland has given the world many leading and pioneering doctors and scientists, and most of them built their careers by honest means. One of those was James Young Simpson (1811-1870), who pioneered the use of CHLOROFORM (trichloromethane) as a general anaesthetic.

A few drops of chloroform on a cloth held over the nose and mouth would immediately knock a patient into a deep sleep while the surgeons performed an operation. Chloroform, in its early days, was regarded by ordinary people with a superstitious wonder and awe. There follows an actual advertisement from the Glasgow Herald (October 9 1848), announcing a magic stage act with chloroform as a prop (the bad spelling and grammar are just as they appeared):

119

MONTEITH ROOMS, BUCHANAN STREET.

LAST WEEK BUT ONE, OF THE
EXTRAORDINARY
PERFORMANCES OF
PROFESSOR J.H. ANDERSON

His engagements in the North cause him to finish his
season of Wonderworking in this city: it is not the want
of patronage: the Mystic Temple is as crowded Nightly
as it was the First Week! (this is the Seventh Week)!!
On this Evening and every Evening during the week, he
will appear in his Mystic Laboratory and perform all his
startling feats of NATURAL MAGIC, illustrative of
the fallacy of

DEMONOLOGY AND WITCHCRAFT.

for the First time he will perform a most
INCREDIBLE EXPERIMENT in
CONNECTION with the Medical Science,

SUSPENSION CHLOROFOREENE!!

He will introduce his Son, a Child of 5 years of
age: he will Suspend him in the *Air while Asleep,*
in a reclining position. This wonder of Modern
Science is accomplished through the agency of

CONDENSED CHLOROFORM!

Doors open at Half-past 7; the Professor Opens at a Quarter past 8.

121

122

The introduction of this powerful new sleeping drug at a time when body-snatching was still in people's minds caused a lot of fear.

It would be easy, it was thought, for a murderer to sneak up behind someone in a dark street, whop a chloroform-soaked rag over their face, kill them, and sell their body to a medical lab.

Certainly there were stories. Rumours went about that people were being knocked out with chloroform and going missing, especially around the dark lanes and alleys near the bottom of Saltmarket, south of Glasgow Cross, and people were advised to take care, especially if they were alone.

However, there is no proof that this type of murder actually happened. It may just be what we call an urban legend. But, after the Burke and Hare scandal, it is easy to see why people were scared.

Chapter 9 :
Sawney Bean

Just two and a half miles south of the village of Lendalfoot, near Girvan, you can visit a cave with a macabre history. Lendalfoot is all holiday homes, caravan sites and picnic areas today but, 600 years ago, if you had been in the vicinity, the cave-dwelling Bean family might have had YOU for a picnic!

SOCIETY IN THE 1400S
In Scotland in the 1400s, like in other European countries at that time, if you were born a noble, you remained one till you died. If you were born a serf (a peasant slave), you remained a serf. If you were a person with a successful trade, you could become a rich burgher or guild-master but, all in all, there were few opportunities to 'better yourself' for poor and uneducated men and women. While the poor ate porridge, the rich ate meat.

MEET THE BEANS
Alexander (known as 'Sawney', a corrupt form of 'Sandy' – short for Alexander) Bean was born in East Lothian, about eight or nine miles east of Edinburgh, in the reign of Scotland's King James I.

Bean's dad (a poor porridge-eater) looked after hedges and ditches for a living.

A lazy, idle fellow, Sawney Bean left home seeking a living without having to work for it.

After begging his way right across Scotland, Sawney arrived on the coast of Galloway in the South West. Here he met his partner.

So they lived in a cave right down by the sea in a lonely and remote area of the coast and kept a lookout for any defenceless travellers or passers-by in the area. They would rob them, kill them and eat them. They would cook or pickle body parts and throw the bones into the sea, to be washed up along the coast.

They never went into town or met other people
except to butcher them, and human flesh was their
only means of sustenance. Their cave came to a
dead-end nearly a mile underground and, when the
tide came in, the water flooded the cave for two
hundred yards. People must have passed the
entrance and thought that no human beings would
live in such a dark, horrible place.

DINNERTIME

Anyone unfortunate enough to be trapped near the Beans (or, even more terrifying, to wake up in their cave) could expect no mercy, because the Beans had no feelings for other people. Outsiders were seen as a source of food, nothing more. Dinner on legs. (And even the legs didn't stay on the victims for very long).

FAMILY

Over the years, the Bean family grew. Sawney became chief of a whole cannibal clan of 48 members. The whole tribe participated in the hunt for human flesh, some keeping lookout, others attacking. They were the ultimate dysfunctional family.

SUSPICIONS

But people were alarmed. For 25 years locals, strangers and travellers of all ages had gone missing in the area ... and bones ... human bones kept being washed up on the seashore.

When the news reached the offices of the King, spies were sent to investigate these disappearances.

The investigations didn't go too well. Innocent people were wrongly accused and executed. One of the King's own investigators himself ended up on the Beans' cooking fire.

The exact number of people (including children) that the savage Beans ate is unknown, but it is reckoned to be over a thousand. No wonder people were scared.

132

CAUGHT!

The Beans didn't always cook or pickle their victims before eating them, and this was to lead to their capture.

One time they attacked a couple riding home from a fair. They cut the woman's throat in front of her husband and the vampire-like Bean women immediately drank her blood. The man fought for his life and would have been savagely killed too but, luckily, some passing locals saw the scene and came to the rescue, so the Bean Clan ran off.

After the poor husband (who must have been haunted by the memory for the rest of his life) gave a testimony to magistrates, the King himself led an army of 400 men to scour the area. They found the 48-strong Bean Clan hiding in their cave, surrounded by human carcasses, dried or pickled body parts and piles of stolen jewellery, money and clothes which they would never use.

The Beans, after fighting and struggling like insane demons, were subdued and taken in chains to Edinburgh, where the Bean men were executed without trial. The Bean women were burned at the stake.

134

Chapter 10 : Madeleine Smith

A Tale of Love and Poison

A GLASGOW 'IT' GIRL

Madeleine Smith (1835-1928) was the daughter of a wealthy Glasgow-based architect. After a private girls' school education in England, she returned to Glasgow to mix in upper social circles to find a suitable partner. She was beautiful, intelligent, 18 years old and headstrong. She certainly caught the lads' eyes at dances, balls, dinners, concerts and nights at the theatre. She soon found herself a boyfriend, but not from the posh circles in which she moved.

BOYFRIEND

Her boyfriend, Emile L'Angelier, was a humble clerk who worked for a seed merchant. Born in Jersey (his dad was French), he liked to dress like a swell and pretend to be of French aristocratic background. He bragged and boasted a lot and people thought of him as big-headed, though he possibly felt inadequate underneath it all and tried to seem impressive. We'll never know. Anyway, he wanted to marry 'up', to find a woman of high social standing and to marry her, probably for status rather than money. He soon heard of the gorgeous Madeleine and watched for her as she took her daily walk with her friend along a certain street every day.

Supported by a colleague from work, Emile stopped Madeleine and her friend and chatted her up. After a few more 'chance' meetings, they saw more and more of each other, walking together in parks, and they soon developed a passionate relationship.

Maddie's Daddy, did not approve of the relationship.

SECRET LOVE

He didn't want to see his daughter marry a poor clerk who couldn't support her lifestyle. He forbade her from seeing L'Angelier. But, being a teenager, that didn't stop her. Madeleine (or 'Mimi' to her lover) and Emile met in secret. Helped by friends and servants, the couple met in rooms at the Smith's house on Blythswood Square, Glasgow. When her father found out, he put his foot down even more, but the secrecy of the affair – the secret love letters, the snatched moments of being together – made it all the more exciting and romantic.

Madeleine wrote around 200 letters to L'Angelier over their 2-year affair, 1855–57 (imagine if there had been e-mail or internet in those days!), and Emile kept every one. Madeleine kept Emile's letters to begin with, but later destroyed them in case they could be used as evidence against her, but we're getting to that.

Emile and Mimi continued to meet in secret, this time at the Smith's country house at Rowaleyn, near Rhu, Argyllshire.

DOOMED ROMANCE

But Madeleine knew their romance was doomed. Although she and Emile liked to think of themselves as engaged (she even called him 'husband' in her letters), she knew their partnership could never be.

A RIVAL

Another man, a friend of the family, entered the scene: William Middoch, a wealthy partner in his own family cotton firm. He proposed marriage and Madeleine accepted, but didn't tell Emile about the engagement.

Why not? Well, maybe she was afraid that she'd tell her father about them and show him her steamy letters (which would cause a public scandal and disgrace her and her family). Or maybe she enjoyed the thrill of dating two men at the same time. We'll never know. Was it that she just didn't have the heart to tell him? That seems unlikely, as we'll see shortly.

ARSENIC AND COCOA

Anyway, she continued to see Emile, even though her love for him dimmed somewhat. She even tried to subtly dump him, but he refused to take the hint, and kept pestering and wooing her. They still met in secret, at the window of her basement bedroom in Blythswood Square, where she made him cups of cocoa.

On a number of occasions, Madeleine visited chemists' shops and bought arsenic, which she told the chemist was to kill rats.

Afterwards, she would give Emile his cocoa and, after each visit, he would become violently sick. Finally he died. After examination of the body, he was found to have died of arsenic poisoning. Madeleine was arrested for murder.

She was sent to the High Court in Edinburgh for trial, where her passionate letters were read out in court.

NOT PROVEN

In England, America and other countries, a jury is only allowed to decide between two verdicts: Guilty or Not Guilty. But in Scotland there is a third option: Not Proven. This goes back centuries and can cause a bit of controversy. The public perception is that in choosing that verdict the jury has thought: 'We don't think you're innocent ... but we can't quite prove it'. The verdict can save someone from jail but destroy their reputation.

During a drawn-out, painstaking trial, the defence showed that the alleged murder victim, Emile L'Angelier, was suicidally depressed and also that he sometimes used medicines containing arsenic. So the jury voted on a verdict of 'Not Proven', and Madeleine was freed.

To this day, people still argue about whether or not she was guilty. Criminologists and historians have ruled out the idea that L'Angelier killed himself. The amount of arsenic that killed him far exceeded the amounts in the medicines he used, though some people continue to claim that he wanted to 'punish' Madeleine by making her feel responsible for his death.

He was buried by his employer, Mr Stevenson, in the Glasgow Necropolis under a grave marked 'Kennedy'.

MADDIE MOVES ON

Madeleine didn't marry Mr Middoch, as it happens, but instead married an art teacher, George Wardle, in 1861. He was a former student of the great designer William Morris. She changed her name to Leena Wardle and had two children.

She became a socialist, meeting interesting people like the famous playwright George Bernard Shaw (she even gave him cocoa – UNPOISONED!).

She was the first hostess in Britain known to introduce table mats on a bare table instead of the traditional tablecloth (so if you don't use a tablecloth in your house, you know who started the fashion!).

143

Wardle left her in 1869 (she was too independent for him), and she emigrated to America in 1916. Born into a Dickensian society of coaching inns, town criers and child labour, she would live to see motor traffic, skyscrapers, Hollywood movies and passenger airlines. She married again, taking the name of Leena Sheehy.

She died in New York in 1928 at the ripe old age of 93, her dark past hidden from the world. But maybe not from herself, who knows?

Chapter 11 : Boleskine House

One does not need to be a wizard
To meddle with forbidden arts

Aleister Crowley

On the shores of Loch Ness, between the villages of
Foyers and Inverfarigail near Inverness, stands
Boleskine House. It's a private residence, not a
tourist or visitor attraction (so please be
responsible and don't go pestering the present
owners). A sprawling, single-story building, it looks
much as it did in the early years of the 20th
century, when it was home to the notorious
occultist Aleister Crowley (1875–1947) (an occultist
is someone interested in the supernatural – not to
be confused with an oculist who is someone who
treats eyes!).

Across the road (the B862) is a Gothic graveyard with broken, moss-covered headstones. The road itself was originally General Wade's old military road from Fort Augustus to Inverness for the mobilisation of troops (all part of the British Army's occupation of the Highlands after the battle of Culloden).

ALEISTER CROWLEY

Crowley was an Englishman, but called himself 'Laird of Boleskine' or even 'Lord Boleskine' when he lived in Boleskine House in 1912, signing letters with that title and having headed stationery printed bearing it too.

After a strict upbringing by his religious parents (they belonged to a sect called the Plymouth Brethren) and unhappy schooldays (he was bullied), Crowley inherited a huge fortune from his wealthy businessman father, which he began spending ... quickly.

THE GOLDEN DAWN

He dropped out of Cambridge University and joined an occult circle, the Hermetic Order of the Golden Dawn. They practised 'white' magic rituals (that's when people try to change things by supernatural

means). Crowley attempted to become their leader, afterwards falling out with their former leader, Samuel Mathers. The group later fell apart.

DEMONS

Crowley was interested in raising demons. You could say he practised 'black' magic, though he took someone to court in later life for saying that. He lost the case.

Crowley's interest in the occult had led him to try to conjure up demons with a book called the Goetia, a kind of directory of Demons. He thought that this might give him great powers.

He also used the Book of Abramelin the Mage, which claims to give instructions on how to conjure up minor demons.

When he managed to conjure up a demon from the Goetia or one of the little devils from the Book of Abramelin, Mr Crowley was going to ask them to help him attain power or success, or triumph over his enemies.

149

THE LOCALS TALK

The locals at Loch Ness were understandably uneasy. Gossip spread about the mysterious 'Laird' of Boleskine House and his black magic rituals. Rumours of supposed demons and devils, and a Black Mass (a satanic version of Christian Mass) caused quite a scandal in what was at that time a devoutly religious community. Even more disturbing to the locals were the alleged curses and spells.

On one occasion, Crowley had a tiff with a local butcher, who demanded overdue payment. The butcher then received a returned bill with names of demons written on it, after which he fatally

severed an artery! The neighbourhood concluded
Crowley had cursed him and people demanded
Crowley's expulsion.

'DO WHAT THOU WILT'

Crowley left, of his own accord, soon afterwards,
to travel the world. In Cairo he wrote The Book of
the Law, supposedly inspired by a spirit entity
called Aiwass. Its message was: 'Do What Thou Wilt
shall be the whole of the Law', which basically
means 'Do your own thing'.

151

THE WICKEDEST MAN IN THE WORLD

Eventually, Crowley and his followers set up an alternative lifestyle commune, the Abbey of Thelema, at Cefalu in Sicily, where they lived a very self-indulgent and sinful life. The British press labelled him 'The Wickedest Man in the World'.

He behaved outrageously, made some crazy statements and had a lot of ideas that many thought were dangerous, but compared with Adolf Hitler or Heinrich Himmler, he was hardly the wickedest man in the world. It seems that Crowley quite enjoyed being called his new title, a persona he had himself created. He had always wanted to be notorious and important.

COME DINE WITH CROWLEY

He is said to have sacrificed goats and, on one occasion, a poor cat whose blood was drunk.

It is also said that he made black pudding out of goat blood. One of the Abbey's members died of poisoning, but it seems that this was

GAK!

more likely to have been caused by lack of hygiene (the house had no running water) than by black pudding, or even cat blood, as no-one else was affected.

LAST WORDS
Poor old Crowley died in Hastings, broke and disappointed. He never did get to become very powerful. His last tearful words on his deathbed were:

"Sometimes I hate myself".

JIMMY PAGE
In time, Boleskin House was bought by Jimmy Page, lead guitarist of the heavy rock band Led Zeppelin.

He restored the house and made it his home during the 1970s and '80s.

Although Page didn't follow Crowley's way of life in any way he had been interested in his writings on magic since he was at school. In the 1970s Page owned an occult bookshop and publishers called Equinox and went on to own the second-largest collection of Crowley books in the world.

Page composed and recorded some material for the musical score of an early version of a film called *Lucifer Rising* by an avant-garde film-maker called Kenneth Anger who also had a fascination with Crowley.

Page made a cameo appearance in the film staring at Crowley's photo. In the Led Zeppelin film, *The Song Remains the Same*, there is a 'hermit' scene with Page, filmed on location at Boleskine.

NEW OWNERS
Afterwards, the house passed into new ownership. The window through which Crowley once summoned demonic spirits was walled over. It is a pleasant and unobtrusive place today. To look at, you'd never know that the Laird of Boleskine, once raised demons, fears and locals' eyebrows there.

Chapter 12 : The Glencoe Massacre

On the road to Fort William from the south (the A 82), you'll come to the Pass of Glencoe. Although it can be dangerous in winter (snow can block roads and cut off communication), it is a beautiful pass through some of Scotland's best hills for climbing: the Three Sisters, the Chancellor, the Pap of Glencoe, and many more. Glencoe village itself is a pleasant spot and a stopping-point for motorists, visitors and travellers.

But on the night of the February 12 1692, it was not a very pleasant place to be at all. Far from it. For this was the scene of Scotland's most famous and terrible mass murder: the Glencoe Massacre.

JACOBITES

King William III was worried about Jacobites – supporters of James II, his rival for the throne, who claimed to be rightful King of Scotland and England. James had been toppled from power by William's supporters, and he wanted his throne back.

So William was nervous. To make sure he had the chiefs of the Highland Clans on his side (rumour had it that their loyalty might be a bit dodgy), William passed a proclamation that all Clan Chiefs must sign an oath of loyal support to him.

They had until January 1 to sign, and they did. The Chief of the MacDonalds of Glencoe turned up at the last moment on New Year's Eve to see the Governor at Fort William. But the Governor told him that he himself couldn't administer it now and to take it to the Sherrif-Depute at Inverary. By the time MacDonald got to Inverary, already officially late, the Depute wasn't even there!

AN EXAMPLE

King William wanted to make an example of the MacDonalds, a warning to any would-be troublesome Highlanders. Old MacDonald (and his farm, and his Clan too) would pay the price in blood for simply not moving fast enough.

A macabre secret mission was prepared, and the Clan Campbell (traditional enemies of the MacDonalds) were selected for the job.

DECEPTION

Accompanied by government soldiers, the Campbells turned up at Glencoe, posing as peaceful visitors come to put aside old differences.

The Campbells were welcomed into the MacDonald homes. But little did the MacDonalds know that the Campbells had been ordered to kill every MacDonald under 70 years old in sight!

And so, on the night of the February 12, the Campbells and redcoat troops, with their dirks, daggers, claymores, swords and muskets, got to work.

In the middle of the night, they began murdering the sleeping MacDonald families in their beds.

The Chief was shot in the back as he got out of bed and his wife had her rings pulled from her fingers by her attackers, using their teeth.

Families trying to run away from the scene were gunned down by rifle fire from troops waiting outside.

The village was torched, the MacDonalds' homes burned and their cattle driven out into the hills.

Out of a population of 150, 38 were killed outright, but even more died in freezing conditions in the hills after managing to escape the blades and bullets. Remember that the Highlands in winter can be a lonely, desolate and potentially deadly place. Lost in the blinding snow, the fleeing MacDonalds died of starvation and exposure to the blizzards.

Chapter 13 :
The Kelpie

Of course you have. Everyone has heard of Nessie, who always seems to be glimpsed once a year just before the start of the tourist season. Loch Morar is supposed to have a monster too. Morag, she's called.

SAINT COLUMBA

The legend of the Loch Ness Monster goes back to the 6th century, while Saint Columba was touring the Highlands to convert the locals to Christianity. Saint Columba is the patron saint of Glasgow.

Originally from Ireland, he trained as a priest, then sailed up to a spot on the Clyde which he called *Glas Chu*, the 'Dear Green Place', which is now dear old Glasgow. He went around Scotland spreading the new religion, replacing Celtic Paganism with Celtic Christianity, though pagan folklore and legends would live on, such as the Kelpie (which we're coming to shortly).

Anyway, Columba and his team arrived at Loch Ness and, according to a report written by one of his scribes, the saint sent one of the monks in the group to wade out to fetch a boat.

Suddenly there appeared a terrifying beast which threatened the monk, so Columba called from the shore:

'GO NO FURTHER, NOR TOUCH THE MAN!'

Nessie took the hint, and swam off. Since then, many people have claimed to have spotted a large, unidentified creature swimming in the black, peaty water of the loch.

LOCH MONSTER!

Many of Scotland's lochs, rivers and watery places have legends of terrible beasts associated with them but, unlike Nessie or Morag, these are not supposedly flesh-and-blood animals, but supernatural beings, phantom creatures that take animal form, usually appearing as a horse. This fearsome phantom horse is known as the KELPIE. Strictly speaking, the Kelpie haunts rivers. A particular type of Kelpie, the EACH UISGE – pronounced 'ech ooshka' (water horse) haunts lochs. Some Scottish lochs are haunted by the Each

Uisge more than others. Loch Coruisk in Skye, for example, is well known for sightings of this awful apparition.

ROAST DINNER!

The Kelpie or the Each Uisge, like many a creature from the pagan Otherworld, is a deceitful spirit, ready to trick its victims and carry them to their death and their souls to the Land of Sibh. They also eat sheep and cattle, and can be tempted from the water by the smell of roasting meat.

A blacksmith's daughter in Raasay was killed by a Kelpie, so her father made some red-hot hooks and lured the beast by roasting a sheep. When the Kelpie came ashore, he and his son rammed the hooks into it, making it dissolve into jelly.

LONE TRAVELLERS BEWARE

In the days before proper roads in the Highlands (even today, roads there are few and far between), people had to cross miles of hills, moors and mountains to get from place to place. And sometimes they might meet their end crossing a river or stream. When their drowned body was found, it would be said that they had been taken by a Kelpie.

On a dark night, the lonely, weary traveller, tired and lost, would suddenly meet a beautiful white horse standing by the water. The horse would appear tame and friendly, and the wayward traveller would gratefully climb on to its back and begin to ride through the night.

Suddenly, the horse would go out of control, carrying its rider off at a terrific speed, diving into the river. Its appearance would change to that of a nightmare steed with flared nostrils, wildly flying mane and mad, wide-staring eyes. It would pull back its lips in a grimace of death, showing its teeth in a display of manic rage.

As the victim would try to get away, the Kelpie would thrash about and drag them to the deepest part of the river or loch, forcing them under the surface to drown them.

John MacInnes's Loch, near Glenelg, is named after a man said to have been drowned in the loch by a Kelpie.

THE ONES THAT GOT AWAY

Yet legend has it that some people have got away, managing to swim away from the horror horse to the safety of the riverbank or loch shore, living to tell the tale and describe what they saw.

Even better, it is said that there is a way to overcome and actually control the Kelpie. By obtaining a Kelpie's bridle (in which its shape-shifting power is said to reside), it is possible to control and tame the ghostly beast and to ride it to any destination. Quickly too, as it has the strength of ten horses.

The Clan MacGregor are said to have once possessed a Kelpie's bridle which was handed down through the generations after a clan member saved himself from the dreaded Kelpie of Loch Slochd.

A HELPFUL KELPIE

There is an Australian breed of sheepdog called a Kelpie, partly of Scottish descent. Able to withstand the tough conditions of the Aussie bush, it's used to round up cattle as well as sheep and is able to leap on the backs of cows and leap from cow to cow!

So, one way or another, Kelpies can be useful.

Chapter 14 : Torture & Punishment

WILLIAM WALLACE

People were not very nice to each other long ago. When William Wallace led the Scottish uprising against English rule in 1296, the English King Edward I was determined to make an example of him. When Wallace was captured nine years later, he was hung until not quite dead, drawn (stretched by ropes), then was cut into pieces. As if that wasn't enough, he had to do community service as well. Parts of his body were used as public warnings. His head was stuck on a spike over Westminster Bridge and his arms and legs were spiked and put on public display in other cities, namely York, Newcastle, Edinburgh and Aberdeen.

RELIGIOUS WAR

Centuries later in the 1500s (by which time
Scotland was independent again), there was a lot
of religious civil war between the Catholics and the
Protestants (the Catholics said that the Pope in
Rome should be Scotland's religious leader; the
Protestants wanted the Scottish Church to be
independent of the Pope). People set fire to one
another. George Wishart, a Protestant martyr,
was burned at the stake in the street outside
St Andrews Cathedral by Cardinal Beaton.

THE BOTTLE DUNGEON

Meanwhile, a special prison was created round the
corner inside St Andrews Castle for enemies of the
Catholic Church and Queen Mary: The Bottle
Dungeon. It was
completely escape-proof
because there was no
door. The only way in or
out was through a hole
in the roof. Prisoners
were thrown into this, to
fall several feet through
the air and lie with
broken bones on the

stone floor in the darkness. You can still see the Bottle Dungeon today if you visit St Andrews Castle.

ROYALISTS AND COVENANTERS

A hundred years further on, the Scots were once again at each other's throats, this time it was Protestants fighting other Protestants. On one side were the Royalists, who supported King Charles and his call for bishops to be introduced to the Church of Scotland; on the other side the Covenanters, who disagreed with the King and didn't want bishops. Covenanters held secret prayer meetings in the hills and if the Royalists caught them, they were shown no mercy. One Covenanter woman, Mary Affleck, was captured by Royalists and had her fingers burned over a fire until the bones were bare and black – a common punishment at that time.

GENERAL TAM DALYELL

The leader of the Royalist forces and scourge of the Covenanters was General Tam Dalyell (1599-1685) who, it is said, brought special thumbscrews into Scotland from Russia for use on his victims. Furthermore, the Covenanters swore that 'Bloody Tam' was a Satanist in league with the Devil.

At The Binns, a castle near Blackness, West
Lothian, you can see Tam's Satanic goblet, spoon
and even a pack of cards with which he is
supposed to have played against Satan. When Tam
won, the Devil threw a marble table at him, but
missed. The broken table can also be seen at The
Binns.

At the Old Parish Church at Hamilton you can see
a stone carving of four heads severed at the neck,
where the heads of four Covenanters are buried
after being lopped off in 1666 (the rest of their
bodies are buried in Edinburgh).

JOUGS

Beheading was a common punishment for major
offences in Scotland for centuries while, for minor
offences, you could expect to be clapped in the
JOUGS – an iron collar chained to an outside wall.
People were then allowed to shout or throw filth
at you. At Fenwick Church, near Kilmarnock, you
can see and even try on a set of jougs for
yourself.

THE SCOTTISH INSURRECTION OF 1820 ...
THE RADICAL WAR

Public executions, a tradition from the Middle Ages,
were still happening well into the 19th century.

In 1820 the poor people of Glasgow and the
west of Scotland took part in a workers' uprising,

demanding home rule for Scotland. They also wanted the right to vote, fair pay and better living conditions: things we take for granted now. There were strikes, riots, armed street battles and skirmishes in the countryside.

Greenock Jail was stormed by an angry mob, releasing political prisoners, and people were shot in the street by soldiers. The ruling class got scared and sent government spies in to winkle out the leaders, which they did.

Most of the leaders were shipped off to the prison colonies in Australia, but the three main leaders were publicly executed at Glasgow Green and Stirling Castle. They were hung first, then cut down from the gallows and beheaded.

There's a memorial in Glasgow's Sighthill cemetery

FIRST AND LAST

Scotland's last public execution occurred at Dumfries in 1868, when Robert Smith, aged 19, was hanged for assault, robbery and murder. After that, execution was carried out in private, behind the confines of a yard or the door of a death cell in prison rather than the public gallows.

The first execution of this type in Scotland was carried out at Perth in 1870 with the hanging of 45-year-old George Chalmers, who had murdered a barkeeper. (The hanging noose became lined with soft leather to make it more comfortable on the neck!)

Until the middle of the 19th century, it was common to hang for robbery, but after that laws were changed so that murder and treason became the only hanging offences. Even then, the number of executions gradually lessened. Between 1750 and 1850, 176 people hung for murder in Scotland, yet between 1900 and 1950 only 23 were executed, and only one of them was a woman. The last woman to be hung (or hanged, to use the legal term) in Scotland was Susan Newell, killer of a 13-year-old boy. She was hanged in Glasgow in 1923.

The last hanging in Scotland occurred in Aberdeen on 15 August 1963, when 21-year-old Henry John Burnett was hanged for shooting his lover's husband.

Capital punishment was abolished in Great Britain in 1965, though officially it is still effective for High Treason (i.e. trying to kill the King or Queen).

184

That's it, folks

Inspiration / Special Guest Star

Mr Death is an international celebrity, appearing in books, plays, films, paintings and sculptures from the beginning of human history, usually in his skeletal form, in which he is also known as the Grim Reaper or (to the Aztecs) Mictlanticutli. He makes a guest appearance in the Bible as the Fourth Horseman of the Apocalypse and receives special attention every year on Mexico's Day of the Dead (1 November).

His job keeps him pretty busy, but he makes a killing (or several) doing it. Does he enjoy his work? 'It's a living', he grins, 'Which surprises many people, who think my line of work is a dying profession.'

Hobbies include reaping and dancing.

Writer / Illustrator

Jeff Fallow has had a number of history comic books published, though not on a horror theme up to now. A graphic designer and illustrator, he lives and works in Fife.

Hobbies include taxidermy (using roadkill), creating srtange art and collecting seriously weird curiosities and junk.

His bookshelves are also an odd assortment, including Karl Marx, antiquarian Bibles, HP Lovecraft and Billy Bunter.

Photo of the author and Mr. Death (signed), taken at a party.

website address:
www.jeff-fallow.com

BIBLIOGRAPHY

A Glasgow Keek Show
Frank Worsdall (Richard Drew, 1981)

Glaswegiana
William W Blair (Vista, 1973)

The Heart of Glasgow
Jack House (Hutchinson, 1982)

Scottish Murders
Judy Hamilton (Geddes & Grosset, 2002)

Evil Scotland
Ron Halliday (Fort, 2003)

Haunted Places of Scotland
Martin Coventry (Goblinshead, 1999)

Haunted Scotland
Norman Adams (Mainstream, 1999)

Folklore, Myths & Legends of Britain
(Readers' Digest, 1973)